Poemlets
15

Cherry Books

The 2015 Collection.

FOREWORD

The Poems in this collection are capable of touching a deep chord in all who read it. Most of the perennial themes which revolve in this collection are that of human experience -- life love, hate, tragedy, death, illusion, happiness and expectation. Ultimately, the message is: as long as people believe in love and the possibility of happiness then life remains worth living.

Louis Hillary Park,
Author, 'Wolf's Run'

EDITOR'S NOTE

Poemlets15 is a compendium of richly illuminating and inexhaustible poems, written by poets from around the world, in an attempt to translate thoughts into universal truths and to represent a large slice of real human life.

Happiness is ours to seize or to surrender, as we choose. In this age of disintegration of humanity this is an earnest effort to retrieve the fragments, to go beyond our small concerns, towards a sense of belonging to something larger than ourselves.

May the perusal of these poems awake your quiescent soul and become a truly rewarding experience.

Poemlets will continue its journey through the world of letters in the years to come…

Sheeba Thattil

CONTENTS

Ann Maria Jose

THE GLOWING SILENCE

You were silent,
They told her
When she was able
To creep out of the spell
Of 'nostalgic' childhood.

Alphabets came into her life,
And yet she remained noiseless.
"Be Silent!" the teachers reprimanded,
In stern voices to her friends
But she was a quiet child, it was remarked.

Since silence was her soul-mate
She was gifted with a consort.
Yet she chose to be silent
But had to muzzle herself,
In her search for tranquility!
She began to dwindle

But nobody cared, because
It was her silence
Which was fading away;
She succumbed to her fate.

Stillness hugged her dearly
Her silence had vanished forever.
Suddenly she was missed;
They knew not how to tame her silence,
As she glowed among the moving stars.

Ann Mary Thomas A

FOR MY UNBORN BABY GIRL

Oh! How long, how long, have I been waiting for you,
A long wait indeed!
Is the abode of God so alluring?
Do those chants of hallelujah
Reverberate around your celestial world like a lullaby?
What makes you linger there for long?
My heart palpitates in exhilaration,
When I envision you my baby girl!

Alas! The paws and claws of evil terrify me;
Uh… that blind voyeuristic male gaze
Geared up to unhook your rompers
Pierces my throbbing heart into numbness!
Never, never, leave your glorious train,
To set foot in this swampy land, even for fun!

Betsy Paul

PANDORA'S POSSIBILITIES

Now my words are coiled snakes
dormant in their withering chant book
crumbling.....

One day, this day, here,
You -
will discover concoctions
worthy of creations.

Snakes hither
Lions thither
Viruses, living, and non-living.

Crawling over the earth
with scorpion clutches of love, from
this old witch's
Fire-sprouted tales.

THE POCK-MARK

At first it was a beauty spot
Adding charm to what was my face.

Soon, it covered the face,
the body, and overflowed
into the mirror
equivalently.

And it flowed
from there
To anyone who came before my mirror
To anyone who came before their mirrors

To every reflection
of everyone
Forever spreading-
Heavily, on all, my once-upon beauty spot.

Cerin Babu

THE BLAZING ROSE

A man of sea from a distant land
Was he, who dreamt of asking her hand.
Hardly came those days of court
For in their midst came fate to sport
Never did his love unfold
For away he went, to the caves of gold.
He returned to see his beloved lie
Adorned with roses in a chest
All he had was a blazing rose
For the woman he did once adore.

Oft was he seen in the darkening eve
Loitering towards the lonely shore
Never again was he a man of sea
His love eternal, unknown, untold.

Divya C D

THE BROKEN MIRROR

My heart breaks up into many pieces,
On each tiny piece, I see my own image
Ugly, weak, pale…..Oh! Is this me?

I reflect……..
You are my weakness,
I wish I could spend
All my days to make You happy,
I wish there is nobody else
Who I am obliged to love
I cannot see anything else
When looking at You.
My world becomes You.
My love for You keeps growing
However awful You are,
However grubby You are;

For You are me; and I , You
The thin line that separates us
The glass of a mirror
Behind it, we are the same…..
You know my thoughts,
My secrets and my fears
I cannot escape You
No….. I do not want to.
Often, I think I do love others,
Deep within me, I know the truth
I love no one but myself…….
Just myself.

The moment I stop looking at the mirror
The moment I stop loving myself
I begin loving others
They are worthy of being loved
So divine a feeling engulfs my thoughts
I realize….my life starts
Attaining a new meaning.
As long as the mirror is there
How is it possible?
Let me break the mirror
Let me love
Ah! Let me love.

The images on the broken pieces of the mirror
Smile at me…

WHEN SILENCE SPEAKS

Silence speaks when words fail,
Wrapped in gravity,
Accompanied by peace,
Never interrupted by distance
Nor prevented by time.
Mysterious yet serene
It seems skeptical yet effective
Hatred melts; disputes fly
Disagreements break
And so does hostility

The heart is filled with peace
One never knew before
And transcends the inner self
Towards the divine...

Divya John

SUNSETS AND SUNRISES

At sunset I strolled this evening too
I did stare at the gorgeous heavens.

Notions have altered as we were at odds
Yet, it's the same coloured expanse.

I love its scenic shades of blue and jade
Cherry orange, red, yellow and bare.

It's nostalgic as I see the azure sky
Focus has been tilted all along.

I recall the lovely sunsets and sunrises
Of the Milky Way, the Desert Island.

Is the sun making a secret promise
Of a brighter or a bleaker clime?

It is for the timeless time to will it
And to work it out in a while.

TESTING TIME

Tested on the very first day
I scored a neat cent percent.
Tested three full years later
You failed -- a zero percent.

It's still a tragedy, no doubt
For even with a cent percent,
I'm still the loser for once.
The phase took time to sink in:

You and I failed miserably
As we didn't score together
Neither you nor me as one.
"Rise up again!" said a voice.

"There's no room for setbacks
They can be made miracles;
It is nature's true testing time
To mould (wo)men to heights!

Dolly John

PRE-TSUNAMI THREAT!

At 2 p.m. came the warning: "The impending tsunami may strike at 5 p.m.
The University buses will leave the campus in 5 minutes.
Hurry up, please!"
Amidst the terrific panic, a studious student barged in,
"Ma'am, can I take
My test paper home to show my parents?" "You're going home, dear? Why travel
Along the sea shore all the way?" "There's no threat there, Ma'am; I think it safe
To be with my parents." I kept quiet for who could predict where real safety lay.
The faculty ignored the Exam papers hoping, "If the
Tsunami strikes, why correct?" The Head added: "Tsunami or no tsunami, your mark-lists are due tomorrow."

On my way home, I gave in to buying tea-time snacks and an improvised supper.
I dared to the kitchen for three cups of tea; then "Why forego a bath?" I thought.
I put on my best home clothes, combed my hair, and sat on the serene settee.
Looking at me from top to toe, Diana asked, "Dressed up to face the tsunami?"
Ignoring her, I watched simultaneously the pathetic TV shots of Sumatra victims.
Barely 5 minutes for the strike! Staring at the orange sun-setting sky, I begged,
"Please stop the tsunami hitting your space." The sky seemed to divulge a secret: "The tsunami needs her own space in time, just as you need your space in time."

POST-TSUNAMI TREAT!

The silent strength of the sky overpowered my imagination;
the atmosphere
Paraded no signs of change; I lost interest in the repeated
TV shots of suffering
Unawares, I dozed off. The phone bell rang many times.
None dared calling me
Until Diana voiced, "Get up, Mama; grandma has been
trying to speak to you."
She handed me the mobile. I held it close to my ears. My
eyes fell on the clock.
It was 6: 30 p.m. "Any problem, dear?" "Well, I was
sleeping," I said. "Sleeping?
How could you?" My mother's voice was soothing though.
I turned to ask Diana
"What about the tsunami?" "Gone to sleep like you," she
responded with gusto.

"We've a treat for supper, mom?" I knew she would okay
my care n concern.
"God has saved us, let us hope. Prayers are always
answered," she certified.
"Mom, what about the prayers of the people of Sumatra?"
There was no answer from her
for some time. After a pause, she said, "Be patient with
questions.
We are a part of the universal plan. Do we actually need to
know more, dear?"
"How I wish I knew the pattern of the scheme of things!"
"Why?" "Just to pray
In time for the tsunami, the flood, the plague, as per the
plan," I said. "I do love
These warnings; it's a recap that life is worth living!" my
mom quipped boldly.

Harish Jose

GROWING

Eyes filled with tears and a blurred vision
I sat in the exam hall haunted by its grave silence,
Helplessly watching as the alphabets
Rolled down to the bottom of the papers,
Some giggling and some roaring
Others with a stereotyped sympathy.

The day of trial for an eighth- grader
The unspoken pain of losing alphabets…

Today I lost my alphabets
Tomorrow my words
Then sentences…, I fear
Life is becoming a measuring rod
Between the interlude
Of losing alphabets, words and sentences.

When I watch them slipping away
I suspect I am growing silent.

Jos Poonolly

OMG

Is it that you really don't care
Or is it beyond your power
To stop all these sufferings
Inflicted in us in your name?
But if you are testing our will,
Isn't it you who instilled it in us?

PEBBLE

The water is absurdly calm
In its womb it hides the storm
Turbulence of the oppressed
Tactfully or brutally suppressed.

This pebble I hold, daring not to drop
Even with an urge unable to stop
To create just one violent ripple
Which will render this calm a cripple.

REAR VIEW MIRROR

Wearing this golden blinder
I am galloping like a crazy racer
Dashing madly to tomorrow
Never savoring a moment today.

I see such beauty fading away
And dying in my rearview mirror
I missed it when I was amidst it
In my mad rush to get nowhere.

Joycee O J

THE COUPLE

They have a lot in common
They are done talking now for years
Silence hangs like loudness between them
And when they talk
They talk together
And everyone knows when you talk together
One cannot hear the other
And when one cannot hear the other
They grab their mobile phone
And chat with every other.

THE INTRUDER

The li'l yellow flower danced with ecstasy
As the dizzy Bee hummed round and round
The sweet, scintillating, swaying Beauty.
 She in abundance spread yellow fragrance
While the wanton Bee slid down her petals
To land softly in the hearty cushion.
He emerged sneezing dipped in gold dust
Scrambling up again, teasing and taunting
With mutual trust, in abandon lust.

This game, game and games I watched unseen
Loud, silent laughter I heard, unheard
Standing far nearby where I've never been....
Then like thoughtless Fate I know not why
I plucked asunder the hapless flower
Off her gallant confounded Date!

When the frantic Bee fled the dazed Beauty
When the grey green past claimed the moment
Guilt became torment!

Keerthy George

A GESTURE OF LOVE

I wish I were a scientist,
Inventing medicines for incurable diseases;
But what if my life ceased this moment.
Life is a clock
Which goes round and round,
Unhindered
Until one day it stops like my grandpa
With his joys and sorrows.
But the day came
When he resigned
From his worldly life
To rest in peace
Never to come back
Torn away from our lives
A gap never to be filled.
Life is fleeting
Yet life well lived
Is a dream come true
Full of hopes and joys,
Grandpa's tales
Thrilling and exciting
Seemed to live still,
A colourful and vivid memory.

Life well lived is beautiful,
Though life be fleeting.

Keerthy Sophiya Ponnachan

INCEPTION

Gazing ahead of time
Languidness breezes within me
Expectancy turns its eyes on dreams
Zest creeps into my skull
To embark my quest,
Unearthing esoteric fortune.

TRUE LIES

One fine night in the middle of the dawn
Three dead girls were having a bachelor party
They faced each other back to back
Talking to each other, with closed yellow lips.
A blind woman saw this,
And drew a picture of the six
If you don't believe in my candour
Ask the green frog who quietly babbles.

Kuriakose K M

SNAKE

It crawled out myself, the snake
Over the greens and over the sands, it covered
Until it reached the prey it searched
And with its mouth wide open and fangs fierce
Bit the 'enemy' with its might,
And it died leaving no trace.

NO POET

Seven hours I sat before this blank sheet
Fleeting images I have with me to begin with
Memories float like shapeless mist all around
Resounding within me like cattle bells
Still. not a word comes out of me, And,
I learn that I am not a poet to boast of.

Lakshmi C M

FEEL THE POWER

The one power known by several names
The one power known by several deeds
The one power known through several sights
The one power known through several people
The one power known through nine worlds
Through oceans and mighty mountains
The one power known through Holy Scriptures.

Running to temples, mosques and churches
Nothing but a vain attempt.
Meditation, mere meditation
The only way to know, to see and to feel thee
And you will converse with the Almighty
But only through mere meditation.

Get control of yourself
Get control of others
And thus attain absolute happiness and peace.

A TREE'S PLEA

Oh mighty rain
Do bless us again
Show thy mighty power
At this needy hour
Our parched leaves and twigs
Are hungry for your hugs
Our seeds and saplings
Have started to stop playing
Hungry are we, thirsty too
But not as hungry
As men ever do.
Don't deem us hence
As any of those humans
For content we are
With all that we have
What more have we done
Than swaying our heads
And fluttering our leaves
Singing with the breeze.
We even take in umpteen
What men let out
And give off in plenty
What men do want
So show us some mercy
And shower on us quickly
For we have to go on
Until man hacks us down.

Lisa John Mundackal

THE SEARCH

No creative obsessions
No bouts of imagination
No soul searching,

Only…
The rioting organs
The anarchic mind
The embracing divides
The macabre visions…

A lone traveler,
Seeking a refuge
I walked miles.
Days and nights--
Days when I never saw any shadows fall;
Nights when I never heard the crickets cry.

Only…
The killing ambiguities!

Lovji K N

NEVER TO RETURN

Oh! Your comforting hands,
Do not beckon me again,
With a strange warmth
That kept me alive,

Now, let me reside in my grave,
To sink in the depth of its murkiness,
And to huddle in its muddy muffs,
Nosing into another sphere of life...

I do not wish to ever see,
The onset of fresh despair,
And another lease of life for my soul,
Brutally engulfed in pain...

I'm about to stretch my hands,
And get chilled in no time,
For I can clearly hear now
The last calls for me...

When I rest in the stillness of morning chills
Will you burn your waxed feelings for me?
Few scented colours of remembrance,
Will you wreathe for me?

None but you to visit,
My mossy grave stone,
But if you too think it a hassle,
Wait not then to collect weeds!

Let you not be nostalgic,
And do not weep for me,
For my fingers dare not wipe,
Your lingered languish …

My vagrant days I lived,
Worthlessly among the vandals,
And in the midst of that long journey,
Found their way, while I lost mine…

My humble needs, rarely uttered
Were only hazy expressions
I thought you would mark it,
But even you passed by,

So, please beckon me not again,
This fallen autumn leaf
Let me go to eternal sleep
Never to return.

BEYOND THE DEBRIS

The sky is blue again.
The blood stains have dried,
All is ruined, but you remain
Amidst this debris,

I owe nothing to you, nor you to me,
My loss has been, your loss too.
Then why amidst this wreckage
Do you shed tears, my boy?

Sons and daughters all lay buried,
Fathers and mothers all lay burnt,
The innocent lot, have thus paid
So early, their debt to nature.

The willful world and spiteful eyes
Will now lament our fate,
Preserve your tears and rise again
Sweat it for a noble cause.

Lose not your heart, my boy
No one will call you vanquished.
Your loss is lesser than ours
Fight and win the future.

Sculpture this in your core
The last words of a dying soul...

Mallika A Nair

THE BUBBLE OF LIFE

Away into the world
We are sent, to complete
Our own itinerant circles,
And find out what they meant;

To experience something,
Spectacular and true,
The simplest things, like
The sky being blue.

Not knowing the answers,
But asking 'why?'
Falling over our own feet,
We continue to try;

For, when one thing falls,
Another grows, and Life,
So fragile, yet, so beautiful,
Urges our joys to double.

REVELATION

Is this a dream,
Or a dream of a dream?
Wherein the sparks of Divine Radiance
Touches the heart, so soft and sure.

The meandering Soul, thirsts not
For dew drops anymore,
But traces a trail of infinite splendor,
Upon the farthest firmament they render,
Emanating those serene features,
Re-patterning sacred structures,
To forge an inner architecture of love;

From the depths of the absolute,
Beyond duality, Love transcends,
The vastness of Eternity
And the briefness of Time.

Maya Davi Chalissery

A PROMISE

Can I have thee?
Have thee for myself
Only for a moment
And in that moment
Live eternity
And in that eternity
Give thee myself
All and all.
Thus together
We shall spend
Lost afternoons
Share unspoken words
And pour the joys, the sorrows
The warmth of tears, of laughter.
I'll be your soft breath
You'll be my dream, my everything.

REGRET

Between us lay the years we lost
The time we could've spent together.

Smiles never born, tears never shared
Dreams that could've come true
Words that were never spoken
Letters that were always held back
Then torn and crumbled and finally hidden
Weight of the question never asked
Hope for the answer that'd never come
The feelings always ignored and then forgotten.

Between us lay the years we lost
The time we could've spent together.

Maya N Menon

SACRIFICIAL LAMB

Vision faded, where pity crystallized
Prospect of imminent death, dried the throat
Flies swarmed over the lesion
Ropes of cruelty strangled the life breath.

The smell of death, suffocated the nostrils
The smell of green grass,
Streams which offer icy cold water
Happen to be mere unfulfilled dreams.

While taken from one place to another,
And getting counted as fit to be made food.
Where life is measured in terms of meat,
The sanguine fluid testified a mere brand new product.

The primeval days of uncontrolled freedom
Meadows full of succulent green grasses
Stayed somewhere in a remote corner of the mind,
Where harmony defined the bond among all.

Land of gods: "Rightly" they called
But now the naming will be perfect
 If known as the land of Machiavellians
Where selfishness defined every relation…

It's time for a second coming
Someone equipped with a better brain
To master the virile human beings
To make them learn

The soreness of imposed martyrdom.

EMOTIONAL TANTRUM

He, the majestic serpent king,
Won't divulge himself always
Coming out in a sweep
From the dark caves of sleep
He may unfurl himself before us.
Often entice us with his diamond crown
And often frighten us with sharp fangs.
The luster of the gem may blindfold us
Leading us to faltering ways,
They become such tempting sways.

Beware of those poisonous fangs
Once bitten, it may overpower you
Turning out the lamp of reason
Followed by a tug of war
With snakes of emotion at one end
And lamp of reason on the other
Let loose the cords of control
Derail the tracks of do's and don'ts.

Neena Puduvath

X FACTOR

Drowned my identity,
In this realm of reality shows.
Seduced by the bounty,
Spurred by all and sundry,
Aired to be the Prima donna,
I landed the city of skyscrapers.
Being a xenophobe, I dilly-dallied.
Rendered pale by the hooligan audience,
But the 'publicity' stimulated my 'x-factor'
I horripilated them all-
The Simons and Nicks in the audition.
The facetious 'four' sat fascinated.
The awesome anchor cajoled me
YES! YES! YES! and YES!
'IN' I was, which demanded
More fabulous mops and mows
I 'popped' more like Squiddly Diddly,
But my song sounded iffy.
Naturally there were vicissitudes.
As rounds went by, vigilant I became.
Subdued, sleep deprived, I journeyed
Up and down the scale.
For 'votes', I prayed, not blessings.
Flexes and hoardings displayed me.
Being petite, a mannequin I became.
Flocks of unseen relatives queued,
For my fugues steeped me in the limelight.
At the crucial final verdict,
I puffed out my lungs with passion.
'Your landing was flat', scowled they.
'I was lost in the Fool's Paradise!'

Nisha Francis Alapatt

ALONE

Yet another nap?
My cosy bed?
My soft pillow?

Dim lit room
Too cold
Sickening smell
Masked faces
Wired all over
Gasps and groans
Power fails!
Disconnected?

A tight place
Fragrance
Whispers, sobs, kisses

White towel on the face
Pelting stones?
Spades
Falling mud
Fading footsteps

All dark
I scream in silence
Lonely
Alone.

Prathibha P

PICTURE PERFECT

The colour of sunrise, hue of hope,
A bright and bold beginning.
Pumpkin faced the baby coos
Amidst the cacophony.
An ever impatient goldfish,
She wobbles in the water;
Creating bubbles that vanish
With a taunting touch.
Time triggers in her the fury of fire
A Monarch Butterfly on a Marigold,
Carrying the odour of pollen,
Mingled with the sweetness of honey.
A child rises, fluttering her wings,
Towards her dream.

The colour of sapphire, sister and soul mate,
Radiant as the evening sky, secretive as the salty sea;
The surface never betrays the throbbing waves.
A Jay that shelters its loved ones under its wings;
The softness of the feather absorbing all care,
With a ripe berry in its beak to share;
Those intermittent fights and the compromises after,
Spreads the aroma of comradeship, of sisterhood.

The colour of life, of blood, sharp and pungent;
Her journey as wife is midway now.
Lo! She already looks different,
The poppies brushing against each other,
Heart shaped apples waiting for a bite,
Honeyed words and soft whispers.

The colour of nature, fresh and raw,
The cool warmth of the fingers stroking the hair,
A lullaby accompanied by the croaking of frogs,
A kiss on the forehead smelling of talcum powder.
Nearing the destination, her journey becomes tough;
The reality fails to reflect the mirror-image.
Sleepless nights replaced by tearful ones,
The mother drowns in her own ocean of love...

The colour of peace and acceptance;
The hands too wrinkled to cover up blemishes,
The senses weak and frail - autumn at its peak,
The waning moon somewhere near...

Each movement of the brush
A summation of the artist's work,
The colours in the Rubik's cube
An Enlightenment - a Creation.

Sheeba Thattil

DESTITUTE DREAMS

From the cloister of darkness secure
Into the light of life I raced ahead
A venture long destined and desired
Creator's gift for the dreamer of dreams.

She searched and thanked
As loud cries rent the empty walls
Expressions pronounced pure and joyous
Kindled faith and hope for the dreamer of dreams.

Years swept past into realizations new
Misty dawn wandered towards warmer noon
Desires crept in, the destitute mourned
The curtain lifted presenting fate for the dreamer of dreams.

I yearned for the glory of life
No less a mystery in its tumultuous race
In glittering pieces lay the shattered destitute dreams
Reflections so still, for the dreamer of dreams..

DISPLACED

These indistinct shadows from a brutal past
Have known much and have been there long;
They have known India, Pakistan and Bangladesh,
Independence, Partition, the Separation of minds…
I am overwhelmed by a hunger
To explore the imprint on the map of my heart,
To journey into a dismal history.

I now come to knock at your door
From death and destruction in war- torn Syria.
Seeking peace and safety in a foreign land;
Would you take me into your home, dear brother?
Would you share the warmth of your radiant hearth?
To heed the story of hunger, sadness, pain…
To journey through a frightening history.

The rainbow on the descending sky
Will embellish her vibrant colours,
Until the storm blows once again;
This is a story which will never end
More Refugees, Asylum Seekers, Migrants…
To walk the roads into distant places,
To journey towards a threatening history.

THE GIFT OF LIFE

The gates of the cemetery were open wide
In readiness to welcome the new inmate,
Destination defined, the hearse moved slowly.
Watching from a distance,
A grateful tear rolled down my face
For the man who had gone,
For me who would go after,
For those, who would follow us
For ever, in the future...

He had lost his life
But had gifted countless years,
To thankful strangers, whom he had never met.
Donated his eyes, tissues and organs,
Which survived in the new born bodies;
Lives which began when his life ended...

LOVERS OF THE EARTH

Wrapped in a reverie
At the wake of summer,
Lovers of the earth
Delve into mysteries,
Emotions in turbulence
Throbbing with passion,
Gentle impulsive caresses
Forged with desire;

Spellbound and powerless
Through the struggle of winter,
Strange latent impulses
Sweep to the heights,
Apart from themselves
The lingering shades,
Spectres in motion
Resign to their fate;

Sublime mysteries dismally gaze
At barren lives replenished
With a trickle of rain.

MY PRECIOUS GIFT

My dearest child
There is none in this world, whom I love as much as you
For you are not of this world
My precious gift…

I treasure you in my heart
Your joys were mine while we lived through it
Now your sorrows are mine too…only mine.

I find strength in you,
Your love unconditional,
Your affection eternal…

When you look up at my face
To smile your toothless smile,
I see in you another face…the face of the one,
Who gifted me you.

My dearest child...my love…

TROLL WARNING

He has returned to civilized society
From the remote mountains and caves,
To churn out society, into an insecure place.
This creature emerges when you least expect him
Causes controversies and meaningless debates,
In credulous, unsuspecting social media communities.
Deliberately intent on provoking blameless people
He vilifies online users and ravages their thoughts,
Seeking attention and an emotional response.
This felon, hunts down people and haunts them
Be it a celebrity or a regular commoner,
Slanders individuals and posts hate filled messages.
Keeps a constant vigil, spewing daily abuse
Sends threatening messages at a regular pace,
And trending inflammatory hashtags, to abuse the clan.
Always intimidating and hostile to humans
There is no enduring escape from him,
A malicious and inhuman "human being".
This resolute irritant, feels threatened by 'You'
Saunters the social media with repulsive loathing,
Always hoping to assault your integrity and nobility.

Navigate with caution, you are in troll territory…

THE VOICE OF THE NATION

A speech that launched four million views,
Where 'likes' were strewn copiously,
As a bed of leaves after a storm;
When the world woke up to listen,
To the clarion call at the Oxford Union;
The call for action and reparations.

In elation, the Indian media rose up
To applaud this Voice and his skill,
To take on the British, while questioning
The wisdom of their indescribable crimes.
The majority of Indians, spoke in one voice,
The voice of the magnanimous Nation!

Sheeji Raphael

PAIN

It defies definition, surpasses boundaries,
The anguish of a mother losing her sons,
The lament of molested virgins,
The grins of headless torsos,
The bewailing of lost elders,
Is this only pain?

The river losing to inundation,
The night dying to a dawn,
The sun fading to a moon,
The clouds weeping rain,
The ultimate pain of creation,
My words are no longer mine.

INDEX

PUBLISHER'S NOTE

This print and e-book edition took inspiration from the support received through 'Poemlets', a Facebook community with global membership. We wish to thank the Community for its admirable support.

We are indebted to each one of the poets who contributed to this collection and Isabel Sebi for the spectacular cover design. Many, many thanks to them.

This issue would not have been possible without its editor Sheeba Thattil and we wish to express our appreciation for all her hard work.

Sound Vision Media

www.sovimedia.com
Ewing, NJ, USA